Copyright

**Title book: Children's Rhymes
Even at Bedtime**

Author book: Jessica L. Williams

**© 2021, Jessica L. Williams
Self publishing
Jlw7462894@yahoo.com**

1

Children's Rhymes Even at Bedtime
Silly rhymes to enjoy your times

This book is filled with up to 20 silly songs that
are both catchy and age-appropriate.
The songs are short, 4 lined fun-filled sing-a-
longs that you will remember for ages.

Table of Contents

Play Til Dawn

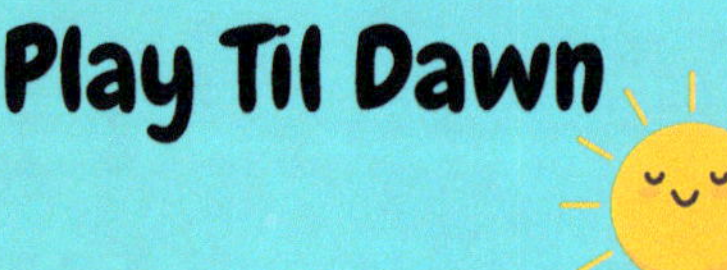

Momma's in the backyard kicking
buckets around

Singing and dancing and tearing
clothes down

We all came a running to sing and
dance along

Now we play all day in the sun til
it's dawn

Ready To Party

We bake a pie and cookies to plan
our party well

There's no more milk and juice so
our mother we will tell

She brings us back some goodies
more than what we need

When the parties over take the
food is what we plead

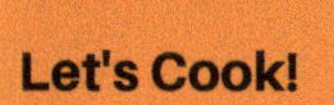

Go To Play

Can we go to the
playground

So we can spin round and
round

Take a swing for a few

Cause that is what we like
to do

The Joy Of Toys

I like the toys that I have
now

I wouldn't change them
no way no how

But if we go the the toy
store

I'd like a new toy even
more

Happy Outside

When I play around all
day

I get real tired my mom
would say

My clothes get dirty
and I cannot hide

All the fun I had
outside!

I Like To Eat

Can you take me to the store to get lots
of snacks

Although we are very poor I've got
pennies sacks

To buy all the chocolate and little
debbies too

If you can't take me to the store then I'll
be sad and blue

Wish Come True

Do you see the stars that's
shining bright

If I said a wish, it might
come right?

Well I wish I may, I wish I
might

Keep myself from this
fight!

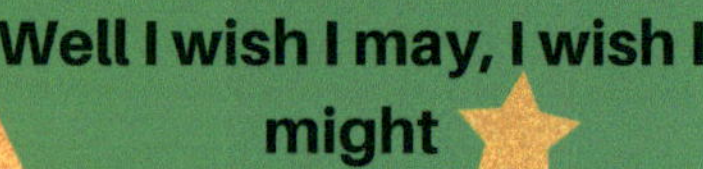

Can I Go

Oh let me go to
mother

So I can play with
brother

And bring you lots of
papers

To take to the
skyscrapers

Doctor To Be

Why do I have a doctor if I am
very sick

Can I choose another I want
to have my pick

So that I may stay healthy
and long life I shall live

For you can keep your
money and not have to give

My Feline Friend

My dog won't let me pet
him

His bowl is filled to the
rim

When I asked him to sit
and stay

He looked at me and ran
away

To Catch A Thief

I go to my piggie bank to get out
some money

It was broke in pieces and I thought
that was funny

I just seen it the other day standing
proud and true

All I know is I will find out why and
who

Animal Look Alike

All the animals were packed
tight in a zoo

I seen so many I did not know
what to do

Tigers and bears with weird
hair

I think I even saw you there

Future Fame

If I had a choice I'd get a cellphone

Not that I need it, I just need a dial tone

Ima play my games and snap a picture

Cause when I get older Ima be richer

Chores Are You

I know how to do my chores and
do them very good

If you knew any better then do as
you should

It doesn't take much effort to put
the toys away

And then when we finish we'll go
outside and play

To Climb A Tree

I know I climbed a tree
today

What a way to go and
play

As I came down I bumped
my head

And now I can't sleep in
my bed

Spider And Me

Hey ma I can't brush my
teeth

I just saw a spider in the sink
underneath

He took my toothbrush and
ran away

I told him come back I don't
wanna play

Food Strike

Mail me a cookie to journey
land

Bury my hamburger in the
sand

Take a pail of water and dump
it in the grass

Then we will wait for digestion
to pass

Family And I

My grandpa took me
fishing

My mamma taught me
stitching

My daddy kept calling
home

On a little microphone

Baking On A Farm

I went to get some
flour

To bake bread for an
hour

I made it nice and
warm

I sat it in the
windowsill of our little
farm

My Clock Won't Tick Tock

The clock has stopped
working

It's stuck at 3 o'clock

I don't know what to do
with it

I guess i'll just have to
throw it on the dock

23

Royal Mess

The king took all the presents

If you enjoyed these silly rhymes or
would like to request more,
leave a comment by email or on
amazon.

Amazon:
amazon.com/author/creativesoul7

Email:
Jlw7462894@yahoo.com